IRRESISTIBLE

SUBLIME POEMS

APAR SINGH

ISBN 979-888521400-1

This collection of poems is dedicated to the energy that I feel. This energy has liberated me, and given new wings to my imagination.

It is the same energy due to which art exists in this world, and every artist searches for. This and all my upcoming works are dedicated to the same heavenly energy.

Contents

Contents

Foreword

Bestowed with eternal youth,
Serenity deeper than oceans.
A lady from alternate world,
Garden full of scented emotions.

Preface

I have always wanted to write something from childhood, which has been fulfilled by my last book Boondein - a hindi poem collection. However, a writer can't be confined to one language or style. Thus, I felt like exploring English as a medium to reach those readers who prefer the language.

As always, these poems are a reflection of my personality and feelings. Through this book, I would like to reach out to people who have felt or are feeling similarly. Writing this book brought relief, realization as well as challenges.

I request the readers to please read the poems with an open and relaxed mind. I hope that my poem touches your hearts.

Prologue

The wildest writings were,
never published.
The intimate love was,
never felt.
The happiest songs were,
never written.
The gut feelings were,
never actioned.
The purest emotions were,
never acknowledged.
The innocent thoughts were,
never spoken.
The bitter truth was,
never told.
The kindest gestures were,
never returned.

Surreal

When we like and truly admire someone life can get surreal. There are things you do or the other person does that you would've never expected. This fresh jolt of energy and opening up of new pespectives is what makes life surreal.

Life is meant to be fantastic and incongrous and that's what being surreal is. These very moments give meaning to life. It gives one a push by willing to take chances, change, learn, grow and see life in a clearer light.

1. Irresistible

Your mirror is the mightiest,
For it can handle your heat,
Each time you fondle with hair,
My heart skips a heartbeat.
You're crazy hot when angry,
Splendour making heads spin.
I wonder if you ever have a fight,
How easy it is for you to win.
Bestowed with eternal youth,
Serenity deeper than oceans.
A lady from alternate world,
Garden full of scented emotions.
There's something about you,
Which can't be put into words.
A certain indescribable quality,
Exquisiteness bestowed on earth.
How can one be so irresistible?
Each time I get naturally drawn in.
Unalike anything, anyone I've seen,
You're a total knockout, killing by whim.

2. Wish

I wish you could see it,
Your thoughts are priceless.
An exquisite mind so erudite,
Ravishing beauty that's timeless.
I wish you could feel it,
There will be none like you.
Can't put it down in words,
This world is darkness, sans you.
I wish you could believe it,
Your elegance's out of the world.
Keep going the way you are,
A flair effortless, unparalleled.
I wish you could realise it,
You're the music of universe.
A playful dance of galaxies,
Driving nebulas that traverses.
I wish you could forget it,
The pressure's that mounted.
This world's an unfair place,
There's no other way around it.
I wish you could find it,
The happiness you deserve.
Keep that dorky side alive,

Never let go of laughter's verve.

3. Desire

I don't know what is more?
My desire or want of yours.
You have my attention galore,
Maybe give me some of yours.
You're not mine to lose girl,
Still why do I wish for you?
You bring out the best in me,
Do you have these feelings too?
A beautiful, cathartic dream,
I don't wanna wake up from.
Never wanna lose this high,
Will roll down like a snowball.
Let the heart tell it's desires,
and mind shall find a way.
It's hard it is to douse the fire,
Can't keep these feeling at bay.
There's a earnest desire to pounce,
And love you from head to toe.
Won't leave a thing to romance,
There'll be nothing left to mow.

4. Beautiful

I know a lady otherworldly,
What a body, the most beautiful.
She has the looks, strength,
knowledge, competence, wisdom.
She looks beautiful always,
No matter what she wears.
Seeing her ways with kids,
Mind goes crazy, my heart pares.
She doesn't need any make up,
Around her I can't help but stare.
I wonder if I shall survive long,
After seeing her play with hair.
I wish to take her for walks,
Look at her in moonlight, sunlight.
Wanna be slayed by her talk,
I wish to keep her forever in sight.

5. Feels

Tell me your darkest fears.
Bare me your injured soul.
Show me your aching pains,
Sharing agony is half the cure.
Do you ever feel powerless?
Apprise me of your troubles.
Why do things seem unfair?
I'll help burst those bubbles.
Why don't you feel safe?
I'm here, let your heart vent.
Won't you let go & forgive?
I'll amend the mistakes made.
Why you fear loving anymore?
I'll ignite lost spark, turn the tides.
Wish you find faith in me, not hide,
Won't you always stay by my side?

6. Ways

The way you lift your shiny eyes,
Each time you leave me mesmerised.
And when you do roll them twice,
I'm left stirred, everything's electrified.
The way you tuck your hair back,
Stylishly behind those lovely ears.
With an innocent look face smeared,
It gets crazy, something in me pares.
The way you walk briskly around,
Like a fiery lioness on a prowl.
Passionate zeal that is one of a kind,
Makes me enliven, puts me in a bind.
I admire wits of you and the chic,
No one so much dresses to kill.
With grace you embellish yourself,
It gets me hooked, gives me chills.
The way your lips move is intriguing,
Surely arousing some strong feelings.
Seeing you talk, listen and smiling.
It gets me elevated, leaves me reeling.

7. Know

I thought I knew joy,
Until I looked in your eyes.
A selfless, fragrant flower,
There's none so benign.
I thought I knew pain,
Until you came along.
Like a lioness you prowl,
None I know so strong.
I thought I knew beauty,
Until the charm did healing.
Like the sunshine you smile,
None I know so appealing.
I thought I knew ardour,
Until you I didn't find.
Like a goddess give joy,
None I know so kind.
I thought I knew amity,
Before in you I saw affinity.
Like a song of the universe,
There's no one so pretty.

8. Wine

You are like cult wine,
I wonder of tastes how fine.
Wanna drink you down,
Can I take my own time?
You come in all colours,
An aroma contrary others.
Every day getting better,
Your ways do truly smothers.
You're a masterpiece of time,
A ruler of all godly passions,
Your arresting looks at prime,
Scent enlivening all sensations.
You did take your time in lab,
A perfection in imperfection.
The more wait, the better,
A lethal weapon of seduction.
I appreciate your savoir faire,
A fervour that's so enticing.
I wonder if I could get some,
You're inexorable, eyes inviting.

9. Smitten

I've felt a few, seen a lot,
But no one so intense.
I've listened to few, talked to a lot,
But no one so appealing.
I've loved a few, admired a lot,
But no one so attractive.
I've been with a few, met a lot,
But no one so engaging.
I've seen creative, sharp a lot,
But no ne so passionate.
I've met mindful, curious a lot,
But no one so affectionate.
I've seen liberated, authentic a lot,
But none so enlightened.
I've seen honest, I've seen genuine,
But no one so damn fine.
I've seen supportive, helpful a lot,
But no one so freely giving.
I've seen compassionate, kind a lot,
But no one so tenderly loving.

10. Lips

Wanna place a kiss asap,
On those heavenly lips.
Wish to take you to a club,
And caress those curvy hips.
When I can't see your lips,
It drives me so so crazy.
Need to see more of you,
Everything's becoming hazy.
When your lips are hidden,
I wish to uncover, cover them.
Wanna know all about you,
You're world's precious gem.
Those lips deserve Nobel,
Even Oscars and Grammy.
Wanna hold your hand & not let go,
1000 years won't be too many.
When your lips take my name,
Volcanoes fire up inside me.
Wanna take your head & kiss,
When you are walking beside me.

11. Eyes

These lovely, dreamy eyes,
Give me a fresh lease of life.
Every time I look in them,
My heart gets feely, soul rejoice.
These deep and wavy eyes,
Water, air, fire, earth and skies.
I may one day drown in there,
But wouldn't have it otherwise.
These pretty, passionate eyes,
Like magnet keep pulling me.
Feel being lost in your lattice,
Sans you can end up at hospice.
Those amazing, philophile eyes,
In them I see in storms & tides.
It's impossible to not turn caprice,
I bet are they lead to solstices.

12. Sublime

An evening that was sublime,
The day was hard to get by.
Was hopeful of meeting you,
Patience was in short supply.
Seeing you makes my mornings,
In heart's vault feelings accrue.
Never waited for anyone like this,
Hoping to somehow get through.
The lights were out, lift was down,
How romantic does that sound?
Duchenne smile of your showed way,
There's a spark with you around.
As always time passed by briskly,
Never enough, wanna see you more.
Hope we find some time, get closer,
Why do I reek of desires galore?
It's great to have you back again,
Was sick of mundane, about to derail.
Next time it's me who'll be away,
I hope you're stronger, won't be frail.

13. Hope

Hope the flowers won't wilt,
By the time you see them.
Hope the sun won't set,
By the time we meet again.
Hope the rainfall won't stop,
By the time you return,
Hope the leaves won't fall,
By the time we yearn.
Hope the birds won't leave,
By the time you reappear.
Hope there's enough time left,
By the time we disappear.
Hope the heartbeats stay,
By the time you feel them.
Hope the fires stays strong,
By the time we douse them.
Hope the smiles on lips linger on,
By the time you come again.
Hope the intervals don't last long,
By the time our feels gets strong.

14. Rush

You give me a crazy rush,
Since the time we've been luff.
It's like I'm messing with gravity,
You might've seen me muff.
It's nothing, please don't blush,
I just can't seem to get enough.
In you I've got a killer crush,
Won't ever let you have it rough.
I hope this feeling never rusts,
Your lush desire keeps me musk.
It's like I am an empty canvass,
While you hold the paintbrush.
The thing is real, it ain't slush,
Sometimes we laugh, others hush.
Waited forever for you to come,
I've woken up, completely undone.
I wonder why you're so plush,
One in a zillion, soul so warm.
Your classy style, sassy smile gets me,
I'm doted on your effortless charm.

15. Love

I am in or out of luck?
I find you so irresistible.
I wonder if it's a dream,
You got on me too subtle.
Having fallen for unattainable,
I keep asking myself why?
Your absence causes dystopia,
I end up left too high and dry.
Never made time for self,
Spent my life avoiding love.
Decision to fall took a month,
It's your allure, made me dove.
No doubt, I've fallen for you,
Did you hear the sound of thud?
Something about your voice,
Your smile's become my lifeblood.
Without you around I feel lost,
You're the one I truly admire.
And until I hear back from you,
Don't ask me what transpires.

16. Possession

You belong to nobody,
Not any one's possession.
Like a bird roaming free,
Uncaring of the seasons.
I know you're not a swan,
And there's no need to be.
I makes me infinitely happy,
Just to see you enjoy thee.
Sometimes I do wonder,
What your love feels like?
Being your lover is a blessing,
To whom such luck strikes?
I am not a guy possessive,
But get jealous sometimes.
Of one's you'd made love,
Kissed in a passionate style.
Could I fulfil those desires?
Of mind and bodily types.
Give me a chance and see,
I'll give innumerable love bites.

17. Call me

Call me in a cold night.
Call me on a sunny day.
Call me when you feel like,
Call me if you're in a fray.
Call me when I remember you,
Cause I do, and I'll let you know.
Call me when you remember me,
Cause you do, and I just know.
Call me today, tomorrow.
Call me whenever, everyday,
Call me to laugh, love, fight,
Call me when thing's aren't right.
Call me, you're my beacon,
Your excitement is my spoils.
Call me without a reason,
For I love hearing your voice.
Call me only for a minute,
If you're falling short on time.
Call me entirely long hours,
When there's plenty of time.

18. Company

In each other's new company,
We tend to find a synergy.
For when you're by my side,
Do you feel this infinite energy?
The way one complements other,
It's a rarity, the pupils dilate.
Despite odds we get together,
A friendship attested by fate.
I feel we shall band up together,
It shall be a never ending party.
With two crazy minds on board,
There'll a dull moment hardly.
Our thoughts seem similar,
Feelings and respect are alike.
In days of joys and sorrow,
I guess our love for life unites.

19. Time

Time spent with you,
Will stay with me forever.
I've never been so happy,
Felt so smitten neither.
When with you time flies,
I never get enough of you.
I don't wanna blink my eyes,
Look into my eyes, take a cue.
Can you spare me some time?
In this world full of uncertainty.
If you find time, stay with me?
Take you away from complexity.
If ever you feel low and down,
Come to me, I'll be your clown.
For I'll not get through a single day,
If you're not happy & sound.
It's as I f we know each other long,
It was you I craved all this while.
This birth, I missed the life train,
I wish badly to be on it next time.

20. Tidings

Feeling high and low,
It's hard do I take it slow.
You're a blazing firework,
How do I control my flow?
Beats go up and down,
When you're not around.
You're kinda wizardly girl,
Keeping me on my toes.
I Feel on top of the world,
Leaving me better every time.
Being around isn't enough,
I hope I am worth your time.
You shine on, radiate, glow,
I so wanna touch the bloom.
You've given me lost courage,
Won't allow a touch of gloom.
You're refreshing, a natural poise,
With you sadness's hard to find.
You lift my spirits, like none can,
If you couldn't enliven, who can?
Feeling high and low,
It's hard do I take it slow.
You're a blazing firework,

How do I control my flow?
Beats go up and down,
When you're not around.
You're kinda wizardly girl,
Keeping me on my toes.
I Feel on top of the world,
Leaving me better every time.
Being around isn't enough,
I hope I am worth your time.
You shine on, radiate, glow,
I so wanna touch the bloom.
You've given me lost courage,
Won't allow a touch of gloom.
You're refreshing, a natural poise,
With you sadness's hard to find.
You lift my spirits, like none can,
If you couldn't enliven, who can?

21. Mess

I know, I am in a big mess,
No need telling me that.
Aren't you in one yourself ?
If you're hiding, shows itself.
Often I end up missing you,
This craving's taking over.
Drinking, smoking, rolling,
It's hard for me to stay sober.
I've plunged into deep unknown,
But you leave things untold.
Do you ever think of me too?
Coz here I am, all love stoned.
Unaware of you, I suffer silently,
All day all I do is wait, wait, wait ..
Keep starting at screen impatiently,
Thoughts all over, pulsating heartbeat.

22. Dreams

Now that in my daily dreams,
A place you've come to own.
Believe me I'm saying the truth,
For you have written this song.
I've just woken up from sleep,
In my dreams there's hope.
When I ask you out in person,
I believe you won't say nope.
Not that I'm your first priority,
And I get why it's that way.
I ain't just another passerby,
Believe me I'm here to stay.
I know you're all tied up all time,
Sometimes 'us' can come first.
In these cold, harsh, dry winters,
We can be each other's comfort.

Mundane

No matter how surreal life gets, there's always a feeling at the back of mind it's too good to be true. Besides, we are so accustomed to the ordinary that we tend to disbelieve that there's something extraordinary happening. We tend to doubt, overthink, lose grip over emotions, ponder about meaningless, and so on.

The highs come with the lows ! Well it's mundane that gives meaning to surreal, and both complement one another. So each holds a special place in the scheme of things we call life !

23. Glad

I am glad to have you,
If not in person, in my thoughts.
I am glad to have met you,
If not on a date, under the stars.
I am glad being attuned to you,
If you're not, I shall never mind.
I am glad being around you,
If not a partner, as a pastime.
I am glad we crossed paths,
Even in the worst of times.
I am glad to see your smile,
Before I leave for the mines.
I am glad we've gone nowhere,
Whatever little, has been spared.
I am glad that you've been sane,
Life on other side, is sure a bane.
I am glad to say goodbyes,
For nothing is permanent.
I am glad for things worthwhile,
Forever is only how we felt.

24. Crave

I feel bitter and hopeless,
inconsolably, madly miss thee.
I deny but it's only you I see,
You shall be the death of me.
I crave you like a small child,
Let's not nip it in the bud.
If I don't meet you for a day,
Feels like I've been mugged.
I wonder if you have the feels,
I try hard but can't forego.
You in my thoughts always,
It's unthinkable for me to let go.
I've waited for you to come,
I've waited for you to call.
I've waited for you message,
You don't seem to care at all.
Sometimes I feel like leaving,
But I don't wanna stop believing.
I would do anything for hearing,
The voice that I've been longing.
This feeling rends me to pieces,
I can't figure out the stakes.
Gonna drink down a bottle of rum,

Until this wrenching feeling fades.

25. Desperate

I do get desperate sometimes,
Being needy once in a blue moon.
I hope if you could appreciate,
Only for you I go crazy like a fool.
Keep staring screen sans blinking,
Hoping for your texts to come.
Sure I do spend time overthinking,
Feels like my fabric's come undone.
I just wanna be closer to you always,
Forgive me if I ever go overboard.
Finding hard to figure out right words,
Just don't wanna leave you bored.
I've been living secretly with my strife,
Having done mistakes all my life.
Now that I've fallen for your true ways,
Hard not to live on the edge of knife.

26. Fragile

I am being too fragile,
Might break any time.
A mirror about to crack,
Reflections don't align.
When it gets flooded,
Baby you're my dike.
I have a pulsating heart,
Feelings are on a spike.
Hey you're my fein,
I am tired of clydes.
Your ways leave me reeling,
That smile ups the vibes.
Perplexed by light divine,
How long can I quine?
When you fiddle with hair,
Shivers go down my spine.
It's hard not to love,
When you're so sublime.
Wherever I may be,
You're who defines my clime.

27. Betray

I don't know the way,
Can't help going astray.
Been always this way,
It's me who I betray.
Cower down to this day,
Left to my own dismay.
Wait endlessly for a fay,
It's me who I betray.
Never did I find a bae,
Under the stars I lay.
Weakness at full display,
It's me who I betray.
Despite all I never gave away,
Prefer fall into abyss if I may.
I kept my instincts belayed,
Today standing again at the quay.

28. Elegy

Sing me an elegy,
For I am desperate.
Mind has it's lost way,
I can't stand this fate.
Sing me an elegy,
For I am in the mood.
Time went so fast,
All I did was brood.
Sing me and elegy,
For my dreams are dead.
Roses have wilted,
I don't wanna pretend.
Sing me an elegy,
For my soul has rusted.
Body is tormented,
All I want is to be dead.

29. Headstrong

I came back from a point in life,
When things had stopped to matter,
I felt left alone in this universe,
All I could hear was useless banter.
Is there permanence to anything?
As the clock ticks in silence,
I felt time's passing' by slowly,
Wanted to freeze it in defiance.
One moment can't fathom real,
Another one I find myself trying.
It's been all failures, wanna win,
For life must have some meaning.
Years have passed like brisk wind,
Never could find my own zone.
Each time I am ready for pursuit,
There comes another cyclone.
Always go in headlong, headstrong,
I ain't a quitter, hope ain't crime.
Every when time things go wrong,
I dare tell myself, it's going to be fine.

30. Renegade

The systems are too rigid,
Society's a garbage heap.
People have turned too frigid,
We must now take the leap.
Let us embrace our differences,
Break down the divisive walls.
These times deserve a rebellion,
It's the fate of future that calls.
People are getting out of sync,
We all know & feel the stings.
That something's not right,
Did we evolve to be playthings?
Who really controls our destiny?
Will it be overarching tech giants?
Who actually controls our fin lives?
Will it be crafty billionaire liars?
I shall forsake the pleasures,
Can we throw it all away?
Let's build a humane world,
Where empathy & love hold sway.

Thank You

If you want to have a word with author wrt the book or any poem, please write to below address -

aparsingh1991@gmail.com
apaarsinh@gmail.com

9 798885 214001

Printed by Libri Plureos GmbH in Hamburg, Germany